KATHLEEN TURNER

A Tale of Strength, Talent, and Timeless Appeal

Scott Penn

Copyright © 2024 Scott Penn

All rights reserved. No part of this book may be reproduced, distributed, or transmitted in any form or by any means, including photocopying, recording, or other electronic or mechanical methods, without the prior written permission of the publisher, except in the case of brief quotations embodied in critical reviews and certain other noncommercial uses permitted by copyright law.

TABLE OF CONTENT

INTRODUCTION

Chapter 1

Chapter 2

Chapter 3

Chapter 4

Chapter 5

Chapter 6

Chapter 7

Chapter 8

Chapter 9

INTRODUCTION

Kathleen Turner is a force of nature, not just a famous actress. Her authoritative on-screen persona and distinctive deep, husky voice helped her establish herself as one of Hollywood's most formidable and recognizable actors of the 1980s and beyond. With a career spanning more than 40 years and a reputation for razor-sharp humour, energy, and portraying nuanced, diverse characters, Turner has become a legendary presence in theatre, cinema, and activism. Beyond the glitz, blockbusters, and nods for awards, however, is a lady of tremendous depth—someone who has overcome major personal obstacles and still inspires people with her grit, tenacity, and unwavering strength.

To comprehend Kathleen Turner's incredible journey is to plunge into the realm of a woman who reinvented what it meant to be a leading lady. Mary

Kathleen Turner was born in Springfield, Missouri, on June 19, 1954, and was raised in a family with a strong tradition of diplomatic and international service. The family was constantly relocated worldwide by her father, an official in the Foreign Service. This nomadic upbringing not only exposed young Kathleen to a wide range of cultures and experiences but also helped to develop her early independence and perseverance. Despite migrating frequently—from Cuba and Venezuela to Canada—Turner took comfort in theatre. She regarded the theatre not just as an escape from perpetual turmoil but also as a calling that would govern the rest of her life.

Early in life, Kathleen Turner experienced both personal loss and cultural absorption. She had lived in many countries by the time she was a teenager, developing her ability to swiftly adjust to different situations. These encounters gave her an inner fortitude that would come in handy in the frequently cruel realm of entertainment. Turner's father encouraged her to pursue academic and intellectual endeavours, but she ultimately gravitated toward acting.

Her father's passing at the age of 17 had a significant effect on her. Turner was forced to deal with sadness and life's uncertainties at that point, but it also strengthened her resolve to pursue acting as a career. Before moving to New York City, she attended the University of Maryland to study acting and developed her skills in several regional theatres. Her tremendous dedication to her roles—a quality that would eventually set her apart in Hollywood—was cultivated by her rigorous training.

Her breakthrough performance was in the neo-noir movie Body Heat (1981), starring the alluring Matty Walker, which launched her to stardom right away. At age 27, Turner enthralled audiences with her depiction of the deadly femme fatale, exhibiting a grasp of both sexuality and sensitivity. She became a Hollywood star thanks to the movie, which also laid the stage for a string of audacious, genre-defining performances. Turner's flexibility and dynamic screen presence were on full display in the subsequent years as she starred in several box office triumphs, such as Romancing the Stone (1984), The Jewel of the Nile (1985), and Peggy Sue Got Married (1986).

Kathleen Turner's journey is a tribute to the strength of tenacity as well as a tale of Hollywood glamour and glamour. She has fought for causes near and dear to her heart throughout the years, such as rheumatoid arthritis awareness, women's rights, and reproductive health. She has been upfront about ageing in

Hollywood, the difficulties of living with a chronic disease, and the significance of self-acceptance. She has been honest about her problems, both personal and professional.

Chapter 1

Early Life and Bold Beginnings

The path to celebrity for Kathleen Turner started long before she ever set foot in Hollywood. Being the daughter of a diplomat, she had an unusual upbringing filled with intense personal losses that shaped her ambition and determination. Kathleen Mary Turner was born on June 19, 1954, in Springfield, Missouri. She was the third child in a family of four, and she grew up in an environment that valued flexibility a quality that would later shape her professional life. Nevertheless, despite growing up in a foreign country, Kathleen Turner's hardships and her strong will to follow her path prepared her to become one of the most recognizable and influential actors of her day.

Allen Richard Turner, Kathleen's father, was a U.S. Foreign Service officer. State Department, meaning that the family was regularly uprooted and sent to other nations all over the world. Kathleen's wandering existence exposed her to a variety of cultures and experiences that would later shape her perception of the world, her capacity for empathy in her work as an artist and her versatility. Turner was raised in a variety of chaotic yet different circumstances, first in Venezuela, then in Cuba, and last in London. Her childhood's nomadic nature pushed her to acquire fast adaptation skills, self-reliance, and a sense of security in strange environments—skills that would come in handy in the sometimes unpredictable realm of show business.

Even though her early years were spent in a variety of places, Kathleen's sense of self was deeply anchored in her family. Although Patsy Magee Turner, her mother, was a strong, independent lady, her father had the most impact on Kathleen's early years. Allen Turner was a strict disciplinarian who pushed his kids to strive for perfection in whatever they did. He was also a man of rigorous intelligence who firmly believed in the benefits of education. Allen was the one who initially encouraged Kathleen's passion for reading and performing arts by exposing her to great dramas and developing her innate storytelling talent. All of his children were held to high standards by him, and Kathleen, who was keen to please, soaked up his teachings on ambition and self-control.

But there were difficulties in the Turner home as well. Due to Allen's demanding work schedule, the kids frequently had to acclimate to new schools, social environments, and language barriers. Strong-willed and independent, Kathleen learned to deal with these upheavals and turned to the arts and literature for comfort. However, she occasionally felt alone as a result of the continuous shift, a sensation that would recur later in life as she struggled with the demands of celebrity and public scrutiny.

When Kathleen Turner was just seventeen years old, tragedy befell the family. Her father, who had been her rock throughout her life, unexpectedly passed away in Caracas, Venezuela, from a coronary thrombosis. His passing created a vacuum in the family and changed Kathleen's course in life.

Following her father's passing, the Turner family returned to the US and settled in Springfield, Missouri, where Kathleen would complete her high school education. Kathleen's love of performing started to take centre stage at this time. Although her father had always supported her academic interests, in his absence acting had become a method for her to cope with the emotional upheaval she was going through. She pushed herself into school plays, discovering that she could channel her emotions and feel in control on stage.

Even though she was always in grief from losing her father, it gave her more drive to pursue her goals. Kathleen was adamant about pursuing her dream of being an actor throughout her profession. She continued to hone her talent after high school by enrolling at Missouri State University to study theatre and fine arts. Her teachers saw in her a unique blend of brilliance, presence, and emotional depth, as well as an obvious natural ability for performing.

Kathleen was still motivated by her father's legacy and his conviction that education was crucial, so she looked for the greatest instruction she could. She moved to the esteemed London-based Royal Central School of Speech and Drama in 1972. This choice would turn out to be crucial to her acting career. Kathleen was trained in the notoriously demanding Central School, which tested her mental and physical boundaries. She trained in traditional acting techniques, learning how to portray the entire gamut of human emotion with her voice and body. Although the curriculum was rigorous, Kathleen flourished in the tough atmosphere.

Her stay in London had a profound impact. Kathleen was free to investigate her own identity as an artist, free from the demands of her past and the usual pressures of her family. She was becoming into Kathleen Turner, the actor, not merely the daughter of a diplomat or the young woman attempting to understand the intricacies of bereavement. Immersing herself in the dynamic theatrical scene and soaking up the rich cultural past of the stage, she relished the freedom that came with relocating to a new city.

Kathleen Turner returned to the United States in 1977, having finished her training in London, prepared to advance in her career. With little more than her ambition and a strong faith in her abilities, she relocated to New York City, the epicentre of American theatre. It was not an easy transition. Kathleen, like many aspiring actors, went through several rounds of auditions and was turned down for roles. She didn't let it stop her, though, because she knew that her passion and training would eventually bring her success.

Chapter 2

Rising Star

In the 1980s, Kathleen Turner's ascent to fame was nothing short of spectacular. Few performers have made an entrance as strong or as unforgettable as hers. Her breakthrough performance in 1981's Body Heat was the kind of moment that most performers can only dream of for their careers to begin. Her voice, which could command, terrify, or seduce depending on the situation, was an unmistakable blend of talent and beauty when she arrived in Hollywood. Turner was instantly recognizable as more than just another attractive face—rather, she was a formidable presence on screen.

In 1981, Body Heat was a huge surprise when it debuted in theatres. Kathleen Turner played Matty Walker in the Lawrence Kasdan-directed neo-noir thriller, a role that left an enduring impression on the film industry from the start. Smart, seductive, cunning, and completely captivating, Matty was a modern-day femme fatale. Turner's portrayal of Matty catapulted her into stardom right once because she was a lady capable of both boiling desire and cold calculating. In every scene, she held the audience's gaze, delivering a performance that was as complex as it was riveting.

What made Turner's portrayal in Body Heat so remarkable was the way she twisted established gender relations on its head. Matty Walker was in charge at every moment, a woman whose sensuality was not only a weapon but a strategy for survival in a society that frequently devalued her knowledge. Turner inhabited this part with a degree of passion that was unique for female actors at the time. The film's sultry, gloomy atmosphere further accentuated her performance, producing a figure who seemed to dwell in the area between danger and desire.

Turner's breakout in Body Heat didn't simply establish her as a leading lady—it established a tone for the rest of her career. She was unafraid to take chances, to portray women who were difficult and ethically ambiguous. In an industry where females typically found themselves typecast into restricted parts, Turner desired more. She wasn't interested in portraying one-dimensional characters, and it was evident from the start that her range was much beyond the typical standards of a Hollywood superstar.

Following the triumph of Body Heat, Turner's next major picture would prove to be just as momentous for her career. In 1984, she featured in Romancing the Stone, a high-octane action picture directed by Robert Zemeckis. This time,

Turner was portraying Joan Wilder, a romance author who finds herself plunged into a real-life adventure when she flies to Colombia to rescue her sister. What might have easily been a throwaway action-comedy became a picture that displayed Turner's versatility as both a humorous and serious actor.

Joan Wilder was the opposite of Matty Walker. Where Matty was analytical and controlled, Joan was out of her element—nervous, unprepared, and a bit awkward. But as the novel went on, Turner's character matured, demonstrating both grit and courage as she transitioned from a clueless writer into a full-fledged adventurer. Her on-screen chemistry with co-star Michael Douglas was explosive, and their clever banter turned into a film's key element. Turner won over viewers with her ability to balance power and tenderness, demonstrating her ability to compete in any genre.

With the huge success of Romancing the Stone, Turner established himself as a legitimate box office star. Due to the film's popularity, Turner, Douglas, and co-star Danny DeVito were reunited in the follow-up, The Jewel of the Nile (1985). Although sequels are sometimes associated with decreasing returns, Turner's portrayal in The Jewel of the Nile succeeded in capturing the wit, charm, and power that defined the original.

Kathleen Turner was a Hollywood juggernaut by the middle of the 1980s, no longer merely an up-and-coming star. She was one of the most versatile actresses of her day, able to handle serious and humorous roles with equal flair. Her ability to switch between a sensual seductress and a fearless, daring writer attracted both reviewers and audiences with her performances.

Francis Ford Coppola's Peggy Sue Got Married, which Turner starred in in 1986, was one of her most ambitious performances to date. Turner portrayed Peggy Sue Bodell in the film, a nostalgic mash-up of drama and science fiction. Peggy Sue Bodell inexplicably travels back in time to her adolescent years in the 1960s after attending her high school reunion. Turner had to portray two different Peggy Sues: the middle-aged one, full of regrets and melancholy memories, and the 18-year-old one, full of uncertainty and young hope.

Due to the intricacy of the part, Turner was able to demonstrate her acting abilities in a manner that was not possible for her in many of her prior roles. She played a woman divided between her life as it has been and her life as it could have been, and she handled the emotional range needed for that role with skill. Turner received great praise and her first Academy Award nomination for Best Actress for her poignant and tragic depiction of Peggy Sue.

The emotional impact of Peggy Sue's voyage was highlighted by Coppola's direction, but Turner's performance elevated the picture above the others. A less talented actor may have made the part seem gimmicky or frivolous, but Turner gave Peggy Sue a complicated and yearning quality that the audience found very moving. She encapsulated both the bittersweet understanding that certain things—both good and bad—are intended to happen, as well as the common human urge to go back in time and alter the past.

Turner's career underwent yet another pivot when Peggy Sue got married. Her reputation as an actress capable of giving complex, emotionally charged performances was further cemented by the movie. It also showed that she was willing to play parts that were difficult to define. Peggy Sue was a fully developed lady who struggled with the decisions she had made and the life she had led. She was not merely a character stuck in a time-travel story. Turner's skill and commitment to her work were evident in her ability to convey such depth on television.

Although Kathleen Turner was well-known for her appearance on television, one of her most distinctive qualities came to be her voice. Few actresses had the authority that Turner's deep, husky, and instantly identifiable voice held. When Turner voiced Jessica Rabbit in the animated film Who Framed Roger Rabbit in 1988, the character was largely dependent on her vocal prowess.

In large part because of Turner's vocal work, Jessica Rabbit, the sensual and voluptuous cartoon beauty, sprang to fame as an instant cultural icon. Turner's sensual yet lighthearted delivery of the character's well-known phrase, "I'm not bad, I'm just drawn that way," contributed to its legendary status in movie history. Turner's voice gave Jessica Rabbit life, giving the character a depth and comedy that would not have been achievable with a different actress, even though Jessica Rabbit was essentially a cartoon.

Turner's ability to fascinate people in a medium where she wasn't physically there on television was highlighted by her portrayal of Jessica Rabbit. Her performance as the lead voice in the movie was a masterclass in using vocal emotion, timing, and tone to build a character. It was just another instance of how Turner consistently found new ways to push the boundaries of her profession, defying the constraints of conventional celebrity.

Turner continued to take on parts that highlighted her flexibility as the 1980s went on. She played alongside Michael Douglas once again in Danny DeVito's dark comedy The War of the Roses in 1989. The movie followed the narrative of Barbara Rose, portrayed by Turner, and her husband Oliver, played by Douglas, as their marriage deteriorated. What had begun as a domestic argument soon descended into a full-fledged conflict, with both sides using ever more ludicrous and destructive strategies.

Chapter 3
The 1980s Femme Fatale

In the 1980s, Kathleen Turner did more than just act; she ruled the scene. She established herself as the archetypal femme fatale of the decade with a smokey voice that appeared to come from out of the golden era of cinema and a commanding presence. Turner made a lasting impression on viewers by embodying sensuous, multidimensional women on television, even when other performers may have performed similar roles. Turner's 1980s career was a study in screen appeal, from her seductive debut in Body Heat to her daring role in Romancing the Stone.

Turner's career took off because she was not afraid to take on parts that required vulnerability and boldness, frequently going beyond what was expected of traditional female roles. She was frequently both angry and hilarious, seductive and threatening, all in the same moment. These distinguishing qualities became her signature, making her one of the decade's most memorable characters. Her influence at this time is best captured in two movies: the fun adventure Romancing the Stone and the neo-noir Body Heat. These films served as cultural touchstones of their respective eras in addition to demonstrating the breadth of her acting career.

In addition to being the film that first made Kathleen Turner well-known, Body Heat (1981) was a seismic moment. Lawrence Kasdan, the film's director, brought the long-dormant genre of film noir into the modern day with a seductive intensity that lit screens on fire. Turner, who portrayed Matty Walker, a charming and cunning lady whose every move and word suggested more than she revealed, was at the centre of this fire.

Matty was portrayed by Turner in a truly groundbreaking way. Turner gave the character a modern edge that made her feel both ageless and surprisingly fresh, even though she was fashioned after the iconic femme fatales of 1940s noir cinema. Matty was more than simply a lady in danger or a simple temptation; she was a powerhouse. She was a skilled manipulator who used her sensuality to her advantage to subjugate others around her with a calm, almost mesmerising appeal.

In the movie, William Hurt's Ned Racine, a small-town lawyer, and Turner's Matty Walker had an extramarital romance. The two lovers' passionate romance soon turns into a murderous plot as they decide to kill Matty's affluent husband. Turner skillfully steers Matty through this moral decline, giving him a seductive yet terrible quality. As the narrative develops, the suspense is only increased by her refusal to give the viewer a clear understanding of her goals.

Turner's portrayal of Matty Walker in Body Heat was notable for the way she elevated him beyond the role of mere seductress. She gave the role a sense of agency and intellect, making sure that Matty was always the one driving the show, even as the narrative thickened. Matty was a woman who, in Turner's hands, understood precisely what she wanted and how to achieve it, all without hesitation or regret. She showed exactly the right amount of vulnerability to keep the audience wondering while yet projecting an aura of invincibility; her performance was a masterpiece in control.

Turner's magnetic presence added to the film's sultry mood, both physically and figuratively. In the sensually charged movie Body Heat, every look and touch is fraught with tension. Few actresses could have equaled the simmering passion that Turner brought to the part. She and William Hurt had a strong on-screen connection, and their performances together virtually melted off the screen. Nonetheless, Turner's performance was made even more memorable by her ability to switch between sensuality and danger with so ease.

Turner became an overnight celebrity after Body Heat became a critical and financial hit. Turner's performance stole the stage, despite the film's accolades for its daring exploration of sexuality and deft inversion of noir clichés. She had transformed a part that was ripe for clichés into something truly memorable. Turner made a strong impression on the film industry with Body Heat, proving that she was a risk-taker who could compete with the most seasoned actresses in Hollywood.

If Body Heat demonstrated Turner's capacity for seduction and cunning, Romancing the Stone (1984) unveiled her penchant for humour and adventure. Robert Zemeckis directed the action-packed comedy-romp that blended humour, romance, and action in equal measure. Though it was a far cry from Body Heat's gloomy, brooding vibe, Turner showed that she could effortlessly transition into any genre.

Turner portrayed Joan Wilder in Romancing the Stone, a lonely romance author who is unexpectedly thrown into a real-life journey. Joan's sister is abducted in Colombia, and to get her back, she has to provide the abductors with a treasure map. She meets Michael Douglas's rugged, roguish explorer Jack Colton along the way, and the two set out on a treacherous trek into the jungle.

The portrayal of Joan Wilder was a departure from the femme fatale stereotype Turner had mastered in Body Heat. In the perilous environment she was living in, Joan felt insecure, vulnerable, and totally out of her element. However, Turner's portrayal of Joan flawlessly portrays her transformation from a shy writer to a bold heroine during the movie.

The rapport that existed between Turner and Douglas was what gave Romancing the Stone its unique quality. Their romantic tension was lighthearted but sincere, and their conversation brimmed with charm and humour. Turner's Joan was more than simply a helpless girl waiting to be saved; she actively took part in the journey and proved to be more formidable than Jack Colton thanks to her keen intellect and unwavering will. As a result of Turner's warmth and sense of humour, Joan

Wilder became one of the decade's most lovable characters.

Romancing the Stone was a huge box office hit and solidified Turner's place in Hollywood as a leading actress. She was able to display her whole range as an actress and demonstrate that she could manage any challenge thrown at her by the film's blend of action, romance, and comedy. Turner had total control over the screen, whether she was laughing, evading gunfire, or enjoying a sweet moment with Douglas.

Due to the film's popularity, Turner, Douglas, and Danny DeVito returned for a second jungle adventure in The Jewel of the Nile (1985). Turner's performance stood out even if the sequel fell short of the original's charm. She demonstrated her ability to blend comedy and action with ease once more, and her relationship with Douglas remained one of the best things about the movie.

The way Kathleen Turner reimagined the femme fatale trope in Body Heat and Romancing the Stone is what made her roles so important. A less skilled actress might have effortlessly transformed Matty Walker and Joan Wilder into cliched roles of the menacing seductress and the defenceless heroine. However, Turner gave both characters nuance and complexity, making sure that neither their gender nor their interactions with men ever defined them.

Turner was the epitome of the femme fatale as Matty Walker—sexy, cunning, and in charge at all times. She distinguished the character from the one-dimensional femmes fatales of the past, however, by giving her a feeling of agency and intellect. Matty was not only a piece in a man's game; rather, she was the player, and she was going to play by her own rules.

Joan Wilder, on the other hand, was the exact opposite of the femme fatale—a regular woman thrown into exceptional situations. But as the movie went on, Turner's portrayal of Joan showed how she evolved into a heroine in her way. She gave Joan a genuine vulnerability while simultaneously giving the character a power and tenacity that elevated her to the status of a real action hero.

These two parts demonstrated Turner's capacity to challenge stereotypical ideas of women in the film industry. Turner refused to let the constraints of the femme fatale trope hold her back, whether she was portraying a reticent adventurer or a violent seductress. Her characters were lifted above the limitations of their genres by the subtlety and depth she gave them.

Kathleen Turner was a gifted actor who excelled in portraying nuanced, multidimensional women. Hollywood frequently restricted females to parts that were either wholly innocent or fully sexual in the 1980s, leaving little opportunity for nuance in between. Turner, however, eschewed these dichotomous positions in favour of portraying wise, imperfect, and blatantly human women.

Matty Walker, the character in Body Heat, was a woman who wielded her sexuality as a weapon but was also motivated by a strong need for autonomy and control. She was a survivor navigating a society that frequently attempted to deprive women of their power; she wasn't a villain in the classic sense. Turner's portrayal made sure that Matty was never reduced to a simple cliché by capturing the nuance of his intentions.

Similar to Joan Wilder in Romancing the Stone, who at first seemed weak and unsure of herself but eventually discovered her inner power. In addition to giving Joan a resiliency that elevated the character to the status of hero in her own right, Turner portrayed Joan with a vulnerability that made her sympathetic. One of the most interesting storylines in the movie was Joan's transformation from a shy writer to a bold explorer, and Turner's portrayal gave it a convincing and inspiring vibe.

Turner stood out from her contemporaries because she refused to portray female characters who were only defined by their connections with men. Turner's heroines always had their own goals and aspirations, regardless of the male characters in their immediate environment, whether they were flirting, plotting, or going on adventures. Turner insisted that her characters be given room to develop completely and complexly in a field that frequently ignored the experiences of women. Her career was defined by her independence and her reluctance to accept defeat.

Turner showed after Romancing the Stone's enormous success that she wasn't scared to venture into uncharted areas. She featured in John Huston's dark comedy Prizzi's Honor in 1985, which demonstrated her adaptability and capacity to take on morally dubious characters. Turner is Irene Walker, a charming and lethal hitwoman who develops a complex and lethal relationship with fellow assassin Charley Partanna, played by Jack Nicholson.

Turner was able to portray a strong, intelligent lady in a much darker, more satirical light in Prizzi's Honor. Irene was a professional who was self-serving and motivated by ambition. She was cold and calculated. Irene was as vicious as they came, despite the humorous overtones in the movie, and Turner enjoyed playing a role that was unabashedly self-serving.

Her portrayal of Prizzi's Honor was a masterful parody of her earlier parts. Irene Walker employed brutality and cunning as a form of control, whereas Matty Walker utilised seduction. Turner walked a tight balance between deadly seriousness and biting humour in the delivery of her lines, which were delivered with frigid precision. She solidified her reputation as an actress who could play morally complicated characters with ease by creating a menacing yet incredibly captivating Irene.

Turner received praise from critics for her depiction of Irene, and she was even nominated for an Academy Award for Best Actress. In a decade that had already seen her star soar to unimaginable heights, it was yet another high moment. She proved once more in

Prizzi's Honor that she was unconstrained by genre or type casting. Her versatility allowed her to play a lethal assassin, a femme fatale, or a humorous heroine with equal conviction, never failing to astound audiences.

Chapter 4
Challenges Behind the Spotlight

The rheumatoid disease presented Turner with an unseen foe in one of his biggest personal struggles. When she was diagnosed with an autoimmune condition in the early 1990s, it threatened to ruin her whole career in addition to its bodily effects. It would have been simple to fade away from the bright lights and cameras and hide in the darkness. However, Kathleen Turner never gave in to hardship. Her fight with rheumatoid arthritis and other personal setbacks would come to define her as much as the roles she played on film, demonstrating her fortitude and strength as a person as much as an actress.

Turner saw a quick ascent to fame in the 1980s. Her name had become synonymous with fiery passion and uncompromising independence, and she had recently given memorable performances in movies such as Romancing the Stone and Body Heat. In a field dominated by men, she was a respected woman. However, she started to notice an unexplainable change in her physique during the height of her fame.

The pain began vaguely, as stiffness in her joints and a persistent ache in her hands and feet. She attempted to brush it off, blaming the aches on her characters' demands, long days on set, and the physicality that frequently went along with them. However, the symptoms got worse. Before long, the pain stopped being merely a passing inconvenience and started to eat away at her capacity to operate properly. Turner would later recollect, "I couldn't move when I woke up one morning." "I was unable to get out of bed. The suffering was unbearable.

She saw doctor after doctor and had test after test for months in her quest for answers. When the time finally arrived for the diagnosis, it was devastating: rheumatoid arthritis is an autoimmune disease that causes the body's immune system to wrongly attack the joints, resulting in persistent and terrible pain. The illness can result in irreversible joint degeneration as well as pain and inflammation. Turner was devastated by the prognosis since she had always depended on her physicality—her commanding presence and capacity to assume challenging roles. Her sense of herself was seriously challenged by the illness, which also endangered her capacity to work.

Turner's early years of rheumatoid arthritis were characterised by intense feelings of loss, anxiety, and frustration. The agony was terrible at times. Even seemingly easy things like walking and carrying a bottle of water become impossible chores. Turner found herself struggling with the powerlessness that accompanied chronic pain as her body which had previously been a source of pride and power now turned into a battlefield.

She was compelled to stop acting as the illness worsened and withdraw from the public light. It was a time of deep introspection and self-questioning. Turner felt helpless against her disease, even though she had always maintained control over her image and profession. Ever ready to conjecture, the media started chatting up her absence. Rumours were circulating regarding her personal life, mental health, and even her state of mind.

Her challenges were made worse by the need to uphold her image in a field that was preoccupied with youth and beauty. After all, Hollywood wasn't very patient with ageing actresses and much less so with those whose bodies didn't meet its strict ideals of beauty. The tabloids took advantage of Turner's shifting looks to make derogatory remarks about her weight gain and attractiveness. Turner, though, resisted letting the camera's focus define who she was.

Turner bravely decided to go back to acting after managing her rheumatoid arthritis for a few years and coming to terms with her new normal. She was going to do it her way, though, this time. Her roles during the 1990s and 2000s differed significantly from the romantic leads and femme fatales that characterised her previous career. Turner appreciated women who were strong, unrepentant, and unafraid to face the world as it was because they represented her changing worldview.

Chapter 5

Reinventing the Career

Reinvention has always been Kathleen Turner's forte. She distinguished herself from her peers right away when she first entered the Hollywood scene in the early 1980s by showcasing an uncommon combination of humour, intellect, and unadulterated sexuality. On-screen, Turner was a formidable presence, bringing a bold and fascinating energy to every part he played. But as time went on and Hollywood started making other demands, Turner found herself in a difficult situation. But instead of disappearing into the background, she carried out her usual action—she changed. Turner's career path is one of the most interesting in contemporary entertainment, as she moves from the glitz of Hollywood to the passion of the stage and finally into directing.

Turner was a major player in American film throughout the 1980s. Her breakthrough performances in movies like Romancing the Stone and Body Heat cemented her reputation as a serious actor in addition to a sex icon. She was the epitome of the femme fatale, with a special blend of power and attraction. She had taken on a variety of parts by the decade's conclusion, showcasing her adaptability and winning the admiration of both reviewers and fans.

But as she moved into the 1990s, Hollywood started to give women different kinds of parts, especially for those in their 40s. The industry, which had previously praised her seductive and commanding on-screen persona, suddenly appeared to be more drawn to younger, less nuanced female roles. Turner was not comfortable with these shifting dynamics; she had never been satisfied with playing the standard Hollywood game. She refused to let Hollywood's more ageist tendencies define her career, and she had no interest in taking on supporting roles in shallow productions.

Turner's struggle with rheumatoid arthritis started to affect her capacity to perform physically demanding tasks at the same time. She found it challenging to keep up with the type of demanding film schedules she had previously maintained due to the condition, which causes excruciating pain and stiffness in the joints. Her sickness and the prescriptions she had to take had left her with bodily alterations that Hollywood, known for its superficiality, was not too fond of. Turner's body, which was previously praised, was now the subject of media scrutiny. Turner defied the harsh criticism of her appearance from the tabloids, but she refused to back down. She was just concerned with fulfilling her expectations.

She thought of taking an alternative route, one that didn't need the endorsement of critics or Hollywood executives, as a result of her resistance. She decided to go back to her first love—the stage. Turner saw the theatre as a space where acting technique was valued overlooks or financial success. She was able to explore intricate narratives and people there without being constrained by Hollywood's predetermined ideals for a leading lady.

Turner's decision to go from Hollywood to the stage was more of a brazen statement of independence than a retreat. Even before she became a movie star, her artistic identity was deeply rooted in the theatre. She had spent years developing her talent on stage after graduating from the University of Maryland's theatre school before making the move to Hollywood. With fewer chances to work in movies now, she went back to the theatre with the same fervour and intensity that characterised her early career.

When she played the legendary Martha in Edward Albee's Who's Afraid of Virginia Woolf? in 2000, it was one of her most prominent theatre performances. Compared to the glamorous parts Turner had portrayed in her cinematic career, Martha was a sharp-tongued, emotionally unstable woman trapped in a disastrous marriage. She had to delve deeply into the character's mind to explore themes of resentment, strength, and vulnerability. The show was a critical hit when it debuted on London's West End and then moved to Broadway. Turner received high marks for her performance and criticism for the raw, unvarnished energy she brought to the part.

For Turner, playing Martha was a pivotal role. She was able to demonstrate her whole skill set in this role, free from the distractions of Hollywood's petty demands. Her passion for theatre and her willingness to take on difficult, diverse roles were both validated by the event. She felt a feeling of artistic fulfilment from it as well, something she hadn't had in years.

There were difficulties in moving from Hollywood to the theatre. Film work does not require the same amount of endurance and devotion as theatre, which is a far more demanding medium. Theatre performers are required to provide live performances every night for several months at a time. Second takes and the opportunity to reshoot a scene in case something goes wrong are nonexistent. Such performances need a lot of energy and concentration, which may be taxing, especially for someone like Turner who was also taking care of a chronic disease.

Turner, however, believed that the theatre's biggest benefits also came from its problems. She discovered a degree of creative fulfilment and control in theatres that was sometimes lacking in movies. Working directly with directors, writers, and other performers allowed her to refine her performances in real-time. There was an immediate exhilaration to playing in front of a live audience that she had never had on a movie set.

Turner also valued the fact that performers who didn't meet Hollywood's strict beauty standards were treated with considerably more acceptance in the theatrical world. Talent, not looks, was what counted most in the theatre. Audiences came to experience the tale, not to be wowed by dazzling stars. Turner loved having the freedom to devote her time to her work without feeling compelled to conform to social norms about what a woman in her 40s and 50s should look like.

Turner was also able to tackle darker, more difficult themes because of her theatre career. She was drawn to parts that dealt with complicated emotional and psychological topics, characters who were flawed and striving, but very human. She was genuinely enthused about these types of jobs as an actor, even if they were not the kinds that Hollywood was providing her at the moment. Turner demonstrated the breadth of her skill and her courage to take chances in these shows with performances that were frequently unvarnished and honest.

Turner started thinking about options outside the theatre as her stage career took off. She was excited to take on new challenges behind the scenes after spending decades in front of the camera and on stage. She was particularly drawn to directing. It gave her the ability to direct other actors in their performances, mould entire plays, and get new insight into the creative process.

Crimes of the Heart, a dark comedy written by Beth Henley, marked Turner's directorial debut. The 2011 production at the Roundabout Theatre Company was well-received by critics. As director, Turner embodied her signature passion and meticulous attention to detail, leading her ensemble in a nuanced examination of the play's themes of personal salvation and dysfunctional families. For Turner, directing was a logical progression from her acting career. Her performers were able to discover the truth in their performances as a result of her ability to bring her profound awareness of character and plot to the entire production.

Turner's move to directing was, in many respects, an extension of her lifelong dedication to artistic development and reinvention. She pursued directing with the same passion and determination that had propelled her acting career, since she had never been one to rest on her laurels. Turner also saw directing as a way to help other actors—especially women—who were sometimes excluded from the profession. Just as she had done during her career, she was anxious to establish environments where performers could explore difficult material and take calculated chances.

Turner's passion for directing extended beyond the stage. She also started looking at the prospect of becoming a television and movie director. She was still going for Hollywood, but she was going after it on her own terms now. She was actively looking for projects that fit with her artistic vision rather than waiting for roles to come to her. She was changing not just her profession but also what it meant to be a woman in the entertainment world by doing this.

By the time Turner was in her 50s, she had made it through one of the hardest shifts an actor can go through, going from the realm of glitzy lead parts to character-driven work. By doing this, she strengthened her bond with her craft and preserved her relevancy in the business.

She shows herself as a woman who has never been hesitant to forge her path, as seen by her journey from Hollywood celebrity to stage success and ultimately directing. Turner's professional makeover was about more than simply surviving; it was about succeeding in a society that frequently discards women as they become older. Turner took charge of her story, finding fresh methods to express her creativity and push herself as an artist, instead of letting herself be ignored.

Chapter 6

The Voice of a Generation

Turner's voice alone would be noteworthy in and of itself. It is rich, throaty, and resonant, but it also has a seductive warmth to it. She had a strong presence in whatever media thanks to this uncommon combination of texture and tone, which her admirers and the entertainment business rapidly recognized. But it's how she used it that distinguishes her from the plethora of gifted actresses with distinctive voices. Turner understood that her voice was an emotional weapon with the capacity to elicit fear, comfort, and seduction in equal measure, in addition to being a tool for delivering lines.

Her career was shaped by her unique voice, which served as a calling card from her early appearances to her later work as an established celebrity. Turner was unique in a society when women's vocals were typically seen as breathy and high-pitched. Her distinctive contralto made her stand out right away. She had a voice unlike anyone else's when she first came onto the scene in the early 1980s. It was sensual, powerful, and unforgettable—a force of nature.

Body Heat (1981), a neo-noir thriller that required a character with depth, mystery, and seductive attractiveness, was Turner's first significant break in the film industry. Her interpretation of femme fatale Matty Walker, who entangles her boyfriend in a web of deceit, was a memorable performance. However, it was her speaking style that enthralled the crowd, not only her seductive beauty. Her voice draped over every syllable with deliberate perfection, entrancing the listener in a spellbinding trance. Turner's breakthrough performance in the character of Matty

Walker was crucial because it solidified her image as an actor whose voice was equally as appealing as her physical. Turner was a gifted singer whose vocal performance was unparalleled, making her stand out from the countless femme fatales who had come before her, according to directors, reviewers, and audiences.

Throughout the 1980s, her voice remained a key component of her character in movies like Romancing the Stone (1984), in which she played romance author Joan Wilder who is swept up in a wild jungle adventure. This role demonstrated her ability to combine power with tenderness. Turner's voice gave her a humorous and relatable quality that kept her persona recognizable while retaining her unwavering confidence. She used her voice to strike a mix of humour and passion, making the character both an unexpected hero and someone who viewers could care for, whether she was spitting out clever one-liners or speaking with genuine emotion.

Turner's popularity grew along with the acknowledgment of her singing abilities. Her voice had rich, deep tones that suited her for parts that let her play a variety of emotions. Her portrayal of Jack Nicholson in Prizzi's Honor (1985) cemented her reputation as a dominant actor in cinema. Turner's voice was once more the focal point of her performance as mob hitwoman Irene Walker. The intensity of her voice acting accentuated the character's deliberate serenity, adding further levels of mystery to the already intricate storyline of the movie. One of her most distinctive qualities grew to be her voice, which was full of subtext and could convey a lot with a few words.

Turner's voice is generally recognized for adding to the perspective of her characters, who are commonly connected with independence and sensuality throughout her career. She hasn't, however, been limited to taking on a single kind of role. She has been able to play several distinct roles because of the range and emotional depth of her voice. Turner performed in a multi-layered way as a lady who was sent back in time to her high school years in the 1986 film Peggy Sue Got Married. Peggy Sue's condition was depicted in her voice with such skill that it was easy to hear both the mature lady she had grown into and the insecure adolescent she had previously been. Turner's voicework in this movie was especially important since it required a careful balancing act between knowledge and nostalgia, which Turner did with ease.

She became well-known for her voice in live-action roles, but it also had applications in animation and other media. Turner voiced the seductive animated femme fatale Jessica Rabbit in the 1988 movie Who Framed Roger Rabbit. Her catchphrase, "I'm not bad, I'm just drawn that way," went viral. It was a brilliant choice to use Turner's voice for Jessica Rabbit. With a flawless blend of honesty and sexiness in her delivery, she turned the cartoon character into a global sensation. Turner's voice alone provided Jessica Rabbit her captivating charm even though she wasn't physically there on film, demonstrating that her vocal ability alone could carry an entire persona.

Turner continued to perform voice-acting roles after that. She kept adding her voice to more animated films and TV shows, showcasing her adaptability and solidifying her status as a vocal force in the business. Another example of her ability to give characters life through vocal performance is her work as Malibu Stacy's voice on The Simpsons. Here she adopted a sarcastic role, utilising her voice to once again create a recognizable and unique character while sardonically mocking the clichéd "doll" persona with a razor-sharp sense of humour.

Turner entered the theatre as her career developed, showcasing her vocal prowess in a completely new setting. She played the renowned part of Martha in the Broadway version of Edward Albee's Who's Afraid of Virginia Woolf? in 2005. Turner's portrayal of the character, which is renowned for its verbal sparring and emotional intensity, was hailed as one of her best to date. The way her voice filled the stage and commanded attention in every scene, together with the physicality of her performance, enthralled the audience. Her performance as Martha was unvarnished and powerful, and her vocal agility allowed her to move between angry outbursts and painfully vulnerable passages with ease.

Theater, maybe more than any other medium, demonstrated Turner's versatility as a performer. Without close-ups from the camera, her voice took centre stage as her main tool for expressing depth, passion, and tension. In a live context, her voice had to bear the weight of each performance, night after night, without any edits or retakes. Indeed, it did.

In addition to defining her profession, Kathleen Turner's voice has gone beyond it to represent her wider cultural significance. It has been mocked, cited, and copied in a variety of media, including animated series and sketch comedy. Her voice exudes a gravity that quickly transports listeners not only to her performances but to a bygone age of Hollywood. Turner has admitted that having a voice has helped her succeed, saying, "My voice was always my greatest asset."

However, it's not simply the sound of Turner's voice that is so amazing; it's also its genuineness. Turner's voice has always seemed authentic in a field where looks and fabrication are frequently prized. It is rough, textured, and distinctly human; it is neither flawlessly polished nor artificially improved. Her ability to stay true to herself across decades has been the key to her audience connection. Turner's voice breaks through the background and connects with the viewer on a visceral level, whether she is portraying a hardened gangster, a struggling middle-aged lady, or a seductive seductress.

In recent years, Turner has continued to fascinate with her voice, both on and off-screen. Her unique contralto has only grown more intense with time, adding an even deeper feeling of gravity to her latter performances. Her voice is a constant that characterises her reputation despite changes in her career and the entertainment industry. Turner's voice hasn't deteriorated, despite her moving into more supporting parts and making cameos in television shows. Turner proved that her voice could still command attention and provide nuance to every word in her recurring role as Sue Collini on Californication (2009–2011).

Turner has supported issues important to her heart and advocated for women's rights and individuals suffering from rheumatoid arthritis, a condition she has managed for the whole of her adult life, in addition to her work in cinema and television. Her voice still has that unmistakable strength in speeches and interviews, demanding attention as a fervent advocate in addition to being a celebrity.

Kathleen Turner has maintained her unique presence in the entertainment world throughout a career spanning more than forty years. Her voice is what has remained constant throughout her work, deep, forceful, and distinctive, despite the diversity of her parts and performances. Turner's voice has been her most powerful tool in an industry where visual impact frequently takes precedence, helping to distinguish her and solidify her place as one of the most unique talents of her generation.

Her voice is more than just a part of her; it is Kathleen Turner's voice, one that has reverberated throughout Hollywood history and still does, drawing in new audiences with every generation that sees her work.

Chapter 7

Activism and Advocacy

Kathleen Turner is a powerful figure in the advocacy and activist fields in addition to Hollywood. Throughout her decades-long career, she has raised awareness of some of the most important contemporary issues by using her platform, with an emphasis on women's rights, health advocacy, and the inclusion of voices from underrepresented groups. In addition to her celebrity power, Turner's activism is captivating because of her genuineness, conviction, and strong sense of personal connection to the causes she supports. She is a lady who has dedicated a significant portion of her life to making sure that her voice is used to advocate for those who are most in need. She is aware of her impact.

Her advocacy activity is distinguished by its strong foundation of women's rights activism. Turner has aggressively pushed for a woman's right to choose and has always been an outspoken proponent of reproductive rights. She didn't hesitate to take the lead in the discourse at a period when speaking out on these problems was less prevalent in Hollywood. Turner entered politics in the late 1980s and early 1990s as a result of her support for reproductive freedom and her strong collaboration with groups like Planned Parenthood. She has utilised her celebrity profile to raise awareness of legislative initiatives that might affect women's reproductive health, spoken before Congress, and taken part in protests.

Her strong sense of fairness and autonomy fuels her commitment to women's rights. Turner has made it clear that society cannot claim to be an equal place if it denies women the freedom to make decisions regarding their reproductive health. Turner has often discussed how control over one's body is a fundamental human right. Turner's support of these causes goes beyond a mere desire for popular acceptance. Her passionate personal commitment to the cause is demonstrated by the passion with which she addresses the subject in speeches, interviews, and public gatherings.

Through her work, Turner has acknowledged that reproductive rights are not a stand-alone problem, but rather a component of a wider systemic struggle that women confront, particularly about healthcare. Over time, her activism grew to encompass a more complete perspective on women's health, taking into account the connections between the need for comprehensive sexual education, healthcare access, and economic inequality. She has persisted in dispelling myths regarding women's health and in her conviction that women need to have the freedom to make educated decisions free from social or political influence.

Although Kathleen Turner has always been a champion for women's rights, her diagnosis of rheumatoid arthritis in the early 1990s made her work as a health advocate much more intimate. For someone as physically dynamic as Turner, whose career had been based on parts requiring both physical power and presence, the prognosis was devastating. She could have to deal with crippling pain, restricted movement, or possibly an early retirement from acting.

Turner accepted her diagnosis and became a vocal supporter of people with rheumatoid arthritis and other chronic diseases, instead of withdrawing from public life. She spoke openly about her battles with the illness, describing the agony she felt and the procedures she had to have done to keep her mobility and her ability to work. Turner's candour about her illness contributed to the de-stigmatization of rheumatoid arthritis and provided much-needed awareness of a disease that affects millions of people globally.

Her efforts to promote health did not end with bringing attention to rheumatoid arthritis. Turner became an outspoken supporter of healthcare reform, pushing for greater access to healthcare for people with long-term illnesses. Her advocacy in the healthcare field was largely motivated by her early recognition that not everyone had access to the type of treatment that allowed her to continue working and living in some degree of comfort.

Turner was able to utilise her position to collect money for patient assistance and research as well as to promote awareness thanks to her work with the Arthritis Foundation. As the organisation's honorary chair, she travelled the nation giving speeches at functions, visiting with patients, and sharing her personal experiences. Turner's work with the Arthritis Foundation brought exposure to an illness that can be physically and emotionally painful, humanising an often misunderstood ailment.

Turner's emphasis on giving those who are coping with chronic diseases agency is among the most remarkable features of her support for health-related initiatives. She has long supported patient empowerment, urging people with long-term illnesses to take charge of their medical care, look for the best therapies out there, and not allow their illnesses to define who they are. Those who have followed Turner's journey have found great resonance in her message of empowerment, and many have been motivated to speak out for themselves in the healthcare system by her efforts.

Turner has actively contributed to the advancement of underrepresented voices in larger social justice movements, which go beyond health concerns and women's rights. In her advocacy, she has frequently discussed the significance of intersectionality, realising that real progress cannot be achieved without taking into account how economic position, gender, race, and other social issues cross to create hurdles for certain populations.

Turner mentors young women in the entertainment business, pushing them to speak up, take up space, and utilise their platforms to create significant change, all because of her devotion to inspiring others. She has talked about the difficulties she had breaking through in a male-dominated field and the pressures she encountered as a woman in Hollywood, including the need to live up to certain expectations. Turner has worked to encourage the next generation of women to reject the confining roles that society frequently attempts to impose on them by sharing her own experiences.

Her advocacy for women in the entertainment sector is noteworthy due to its emphasis on questioning the existing quo. Turner has been an outspoken opponent of ageism in the profession, especially as it pertains to women, and she has advocated for more chances for senior actors to play significant, challenging parts. She has also continuously pushed the business to close the pay disparity that still exists between male and female performers. Turner has worked both openly and behind the scenes to promote more gender equality in the business. Her advocacy in this area stems from a sincere desire to see structural change.

Although her advocacy has won her praise from many people, there have been difficulties along the way. Turner has occasionally encountered hostility and criticism for her candid opinions, especially when it comes to matters of reproductive rights. She has, however, been unwavering and has never backed down from a battle. Her strength of character and her everlasting dedication to justice are demonstrated by her capacity to stick to her principles in the face of criticism.

The most potent weapon Kathleen Turner has had in her decades of advocacy work has been her voice. Turner's rich, rich voice draws attention whether she's testifying before Congress, addressing a crowd at a protest, or telling her tale in interviews. She is an engaging advocate not just because of the way she speaks, but also because of the sincerity and conviction in her remarks. Turner does not speak as someone who is divorced from the problems; rather, he speaks as someone who has experienced them firsthand, overcome them, and emerged stronger.

Her strong sense of empathy and desire to empower others are what motivate her activity. Turner's efforts to uplift others around her have had a cascading effect, encouraging a great number of people to speak up and support the issues that are important to them. Whether it's via mentoring young women in Hollywood, bringing attention to chronic conditions, or advocating for the reproductive rights of women throughout the nation, she has continuously utilised her position to make room for others.

Turner's capacity to relate to people on a personal level is among her activism's most impressive features. She conducts her advocacy work with humility and a profound knowledge of the problems encountered by regular people, despite her celebrity position. She is a very powerful advocate because of her link to the human experience. Turner's advocacy is based on the conviction that every individual deserves respect, decency, and the freedom to live their life without being subjected to persecution, regardless of whether they are speaking out against healthcare reform or for women's rights.

Beyond her career as an actor, Kathleen Turner is a fighter for justice, an ardent supporter of the weaker person, and a voice for those whose voices are far too frequently muffled. Her advocacy is an essential component of who she is and not just a footnote to her profession. Turner believes that activism and acting are connected because they have the same goals of telling stories, bringing attention to the human condition, and improving equity for everyone.

Long after the last credits have rolled, her impact as an activist and champion will live on, inspiring the next generations of change makers and activists. She has demonstrated to the world that genuine success comes from using your position to fight for justice, uplift others, and bring about long-lasting change—simply succeeding in your own right is not enough. Kathleen Turner has achieved remarkable success in her endeavour.

Chapter 8

Individual Life

Although Kathleen Turner is most recognized for her powerful performances and distinctive voice, a closer look at her personal life reveals a path filled with parenting, meaningful relationships, and hard-won knowledge. She has raised a complicated life that extends well beyond the silver screen while enduring the highs and lows of Hollywood throughout the years. Her mothering position, which she has always held in the greatest esteem, and her connections, both personal and professional, have influenced her. Turner has demonstrated endurance, self-reflection, and, in the end, a profound comprehension of what is important in his personal life.

Her marriage to real estate mogul Jay Weiss represents a significant turning point in her life. Weiss gave Turner a solid base; he was a man from beyond Hollywood's glitter and glamour. They tied the knot in 1984, and although there were difficulties in their marriage, the two had a great deal of respect and support for one another. Weiss acted as a stabilising influence on Turner over his sometimes tumultuous career, and their relationship was always one of quiet strength.

Turner has talked over the years about the delicate balance she attempted to keep between her relationship with Weiss and her demanding work. She frequently compared her marriage to an anchor in the Hollywood whirlwind. But even though they were fond of each other, their relationship started to suffer as a result of her growing celebrity and the demands of her work. After over 20 years of marriage, the couple decided to split ways and divorced peacefully in the early 2000s. Turner has always been quite complimentary of Weiss, even after their split, stressing the value of their relationship and the close relationship they have both before and after marriage.

Turner's life has been defined by motherhood, and the 1987 birth of her daughter Rachel Ann Weiss caused a significant change in her priorities. Turner has said several times that one of the greatest life-changing events she has had is becoming a mother. In many ways, Rachel came to represent Turner's world, providing her with a sense of stability that no position or honour could ever provide. Turner and her daughter have always had a tight relationship that is characterised by love, tolerance, and respect for one another.

It was not easy to juggle the duties of parenting with a lucrative Hollywood profession. Turner has been open about the difficulties of being a working mother, particularly in a field where personal time is frequently in short supply. She has talked about the difficulties she had juggling a demanding performing schedule with her attempts to be there for her kid. Turner experienced guilty moments and times when she saw the pull of her profession separating her from her family. She was, however, unwaveringly committed to making sure Rachel had a strong feeling of love and security as a child.

Later on, Turner found herself stepping into the role of mentor while Rachel followed her musical career. Turner welcomed the change in her job and offered advice, encouragement, and the knowledge she had gathered from her years in the entertainment business. She has frequently shown delight in Rachel's development into a young woman by praising her ability and independence.

Turner's sense of duty to the world around her and her kid was further enhanced by motherhood. She has talked about how having a child altered her viewpoint on her advocacy, especially about women's rights and health-related concerns. She felt a closer connection to these issues, inspired by a desire to build a better world for her daughter and future generations of women. Turner's advocacy work gained fresh meaning as a result of this viewpoint change, and she started speaking up more about issues that directly affected women and children.

Turner's path was also significantly shaped by the health issues she encountered later in life. After receiving a rheumatoid arthritis diagnosis in the early 1990s, she was forced to deal with a mental and physical battle that would affect her in her personal and professional life. The prognosis was upsetting for someone whose work had frequently depended on physique and presence. It felt all-consuming at moments, and the agony was quite strong. Turner's illness made it difficult for her to work and strained her connections with others, but it also made her reevaluate her life.

Turner gradually accepted the condition and drew support from everyone around her, particularly her daughter. She started to view her illness as a task that needed to be addressed with bravery and resilience rather than something that would define her. Turner did not allow the illness to break her spirit, even though the path was difficult at times and she experienced periods of anger and hopelessness. Since she has used her position to fight for individuals who might not have access to the same services or support that she did, her openness about the experience has served as an inspiration to many.

Turner accepted a greater sense of understanding about life and her decisions as she overcame her health issues. She has frequently discussed the value of introspection and personal development, emphasising that the challenges she overcame in her work, marriage, or health provided her with priceless self-discovery. Turner has demonstrated in his personal life a desire to grow, learn, and adapt even in the face of hardship.

Turner's personal story is remarkable in part because she refused to allow Hollywood to define who she was. Turner has always been transparent about who she is and what she loves, in a field where appearance is sometimes more important than content. Many performers have found it difficult to maintain a personal life. She has never held back when talking about the difficulties she had in Hollywood, especially as a woman trying to make her place in a mostly male field. She has, however, always been loyal to herself, even if it meant declining projects or taking on fewer parts that didn't fit with her morals.

Turner has also discussed the challenges faced by elderly women in Hollywood as she has become older. She has advocated for more possibilities for women of all ages to assume major positions and has been open about the ageism that still exists in the profession. Turner's support of older women in Hollywood is very personal to her, as she has witnessed directly how the business may marginalise actors beyond a particular age. In addition to influencing other women in the business, her willingness to speak out on these problems has generated crucial discussions about equity and representation in Hollywood.

Turner's private life serves as an example of the resilience of the human spirit. Her experiences as a mother, in her relationships, and her fights with disease have given her a great sense of insight and comprehension. She now understands the value of embracing life's intricacies and all of its joys and sorrows. She is well-liked not only in the entertainment industry but also in the hearts of people who respect her fortitude and resilience because of her capacity to honestly and gracefully consider her experiences.

Turner's dedication to honesty has remained one of the most recurrent themes in her personal life. Whether it's in her private or public life, she has always been unabashedly herself. She has benefited much from her dedication to authenticity, which has enabled her to establish relationships based on respect and trust. It's also the reason that so many people have been drawn to her in both her personal and professional lives.

Chapter 9

The Legend's Legacy

Beyond a lifetime of remarkable performances, Kathleen Turner leaves behind a legacy. It is evidence of the tenacity, genuineness, and conviction of those who possess these qualities. Generations to come will be impacted by her influence on the arts and activism, as she is viewed as a symbol of courage and integrity by advocates and activists in addition to actors and filmmakers. Turner will continue to have an impact on people's lives who look up to her on and off screen as long as her body of work remains and her advocacy empowers others.

Her contributions to the film industry are unmatched. Turner changed the definition of what it meant to be a leading lady in Hollywood from the moment she first appeared on the scene in the early 1980s. She became known for her seductive, deep voice, but her unadulterated talent and bold decisions elevated her to the status of one of the most respected actresses of her day. Turner never liked to take things easy. She defied the conventional gender stereotypes of the day by accepting roles that required vulnerability, strength, and complexity. She has a dynamic range that few actresses could equal in movies like Body Heat, Romancing the Stone, and Peggy Sue Got Married. She may portray an erotically attractive femme fatale, an adventurous heroine, or a contemplative lady navigating the unexpected turns of life. Turner paved the way for characters with true complexity and became a symbol of empowerment in Hollywood that frequently ignored women.

The way she handled her art shows how much of an effect she will have on performers in the future. Turner gave every performance a degree of dedication that was evident upon watching. Aspiring actors will continue to be inspired by her unwavering preparation and frequent complete immersion in her roles. Turner showed that being a genuine artist involves more than simply playing a role; it also entails elevating the narrative and evoking strong emotions in the viewer. Her performances were always nuanced, multi-layered, and intensely emotional; they were never one-dimensional. She tackled her jobs with the conviction that subtlety and nuance could still be found in popular entertainment.

But Kathleen Turner's reluctance to fit in is what makes her stand out, even with her unquestionable screen presence. Turner never gave in to peer pressure, even in a field known for having strict standards and expectations, particularly when it came to women. She refused to conform to preconceived notions or adopt a more palatable persona. Rather, she advocated for authenticity, a trait that still strikes a chord with up-and-coming artists who are seeking acceptance for who they are in a society that frequently expects conformity. Future generations will be motivated by Turner's stubbornness to follow their path, reject compromise, and pursue their creativity on their terms because she was real and never let the industry define her.

Turner's influence continues to be a benchmark for those who want to produce tales that subvert the current quo, even as the industry changes and new voices emerge. At a period when such parts were uncommon, she helped lead the way for nuanced, multifaceted female characters, and her impact has contributed to the rising push for improved representation of women in cinema. In a world where diversity and inclusiveness are becoming more and more valued, Turner's body of work serves as a reminder that strong, complex female characters are essential and can completely change the course of a story.

Her impact goes beyond the movies she has acted in. Turner's activism has been a pillar of her legacy, demonstrating her conviction that campaigning and art can and ought to coexist. Turner has dedicated decades of her life to promoting women's rights, healthcare access, and reproductive freedom. She was aware that her celebrity gave her the ability to influence change, and she never thought twice about using her position to advocate for issues close to her heart. Turner's activism has been characterised by a strong sense of urgency and duty, whether it was speaking before Congress on behalf of women's reproductive rights, advocating for healthcare reform, or spreading awareness about rheumatoid arthritis.

Turner will serve as a role model for activists in the future on how to use one's high status to effect real change. She never engaged in phony or superficial advocacy. She studied these topics in great detail, appreciating their subtleties and complexity. She wasn't satisfied with just being a symbol for a cause; she was actively involved in the fight, meeting with legislators, giving speeches at events, and lending her voice to those whose voices would not have been heard otherwise. Turner's strong and uncompromising dedication to her beliefs will serve as an inspiration to campaigners who think that celebrity can propel social change.

Among her legacy, her support for healthcare reform stands out as particularly noteworthy. Turner encountered firsthand the difficulties of navigating a healthcare system that frequently fails people with chronic diseases after receiving a diagnosis of rheumatoid arthritis. Instead of stepping away from the limelight, she joined the Arthritis Foundation as a spokesman, using her own experience to draw attention to more general problems with the healthcare system. She saw the value of sharing her story to connect with those who were going through difficult times in silence as well as to increase awareness. Future generations of activists who understand the significance of battling for universal access to healthcare, particularly for individuals with chronic diseases who are frequently disenfranchised by the system, will find inspiration in Turner's efforts as a healthcare advocate.

Turner's involvement also serves as a reminder that lobbying is a lifetime commitment rather than a one-time project. She didn't confine her involvement to a certain cause or a brief period when she attracted notice from the media. Rather, she has dedicated decades to promoting a broad array of causes, realising that genuine advancement necessitates consistent work. Future generations can draw inspiration from this enduring commitment when they set out on their activist journeys. Turner's life has demonstrated that the pursuit of justice is a never-ending battle and that real change frequently requires patience, perseverance, and a readiness to face setbacks.

Turner's influence is equally as strong in the theatre. She took parts that tested her as an artist and broadened her repertory while bringing her distinctive personality to the stage. Her performance in Virginia Woolf's Who's Afraid of Martha? Gained praise from critics and showed that she could control a stage with the same passion as she did a movie. Turner's theatrical contributions have aided in bridging the gap between stage and cinema acting, demonstrating to upcoming actors that the two forms of expression are complementary rather than antagonistic.

Young performers will continue to be inspired by Turner's influence on theatre as they perceive her career as a model of adaptability. She was never satisfied with being limited to a single media. Turner gave every character she played the same amount of attention and passion, whether it was on stage or screen, and her ability to transition between the two mediums so well has made it possible for other actresses to follow in her footsteps. Her accomplishments in both fields show that great artistic talent has no boundaries and that mastery of one medium can only improve work in another.

Another aspect of Kathleen Turner's impact is her mentoring. She has been open about the value of teaching the next generation what she has learned over the years. She has served as a mentor to young women in the entertainment sector, providing them with advice, encouragement, and the benefit of her acquired expertise. As a proponent of giving women a voice in Hollywood, Turner has paved the road for greater gender equality via her support of other women in the business.

Turner will be seen by the next generations of artists as a role model, someone who has achieved success in her own right while also making it a point to support the success of others. Her desire to open up about her experiences—both the good and the bad—demonstrates her faith in the strength of camaraderie and teamwork. Because of her mentorship, Turner's influence will continue long after her career is over, impacting the careers of numerous people who look up to her as an example of what can happen when someone stays true to who they are.

Another important aspect of Turner's legacy is the wisdom she has accumulated over the years. She has frequently discussed the lessons she has picked up from both her achievements and her setbacks. Turner is an example to everyone navigating life's intricacies, not only those in the entertainment business but also to others because of her capacity to reflect on her experiences with grace and honesty. Turner is a sympathetic character whose story reflects the hardships and victories of countless people because she is determined to be honest and open about her life.

Turner is a lady who lived her life on her terms, and that will be evident to future generations when they look at her legacy. One of the things that have defined her career and activism is her reluctance to adapt to the expectations of others. She has never let others influence her decisions. Turner left behind a legacy of fortitude, sincerity, and tenacity. She has demonstrated to the world that genuine success is about remaining true to who you are, standing up for what you believe in, and using your voice to change the world rather than about recognition or awards.

Since Kathleen Turner is an artist and activist, her influence will remain for years to come as she encourages young people to push boundaries, question conventions, and effect long-lasting change. Her legacy is one of empowerment: she has given voice and strength to campaigners seeking justice, to chronic disease sufferers, and women in Hollywood. Turner's narrative is far from done, and as her impact keeps growing, the next generations will regard her as a legend whose influence goes beyond the big screen and into the hearts of those who aspire to improve the world.

www.ingramcontent.com/pod-product-compliance
Ingram Content Group UK Ltd.
Pitfield, Milton Keynes, MK11 3LW, UK
UKHW020624160126